WHAT MATTERS

Adele Kenny

Welcome Rain Publishers
NEW YORK

Welcome Rain Publishers
217 Thompson Street, #473
New York, New York 10012

Acknowledgments: Grateful acknowledgment is made to the editors of
the following journals, anthologies, and books in which poems from this
collection have appeared (some in earlier forms and with earlier titles):
*Adanna; Black Swan Review; California Quarterly; Chosen Ghosts; Delaware
Valley Poets Anthology #5; Edison Literary Review; Exit 13; Journal of New
Jersey Poets; Kean Review; Lips; Merton Seasonal; Off Line; Paterson Literary
Review; Sing Heavenly Muse; Thatchwork; The American Voice in Poetry: The
Legacy of Whitman, Williams, and Ginsberg; The Carriage House Poetry Series
Anthology; Tiferet: A Journal of Spiritual Literature; U.S. 1 Worksheets;* and
Voices From Here.

ISBN-13: 978-1566490795
ISBN-10: 1566490790

Library of Congress catalog information is available from the publisher.

Book design by Laura Smyth

Also by Adele Kenny

Poetry
The Kite & Other Poems from Childhood
Chosen Ghosts
At the Edge of the Woods
Starship Earth
Castles and Dragons
Questi Momenti
Migrating Geese
Between Hail Marys
Illegal Entries
The Roses Open
Refusing the Frog
An Archaeology of Ruins
Notes from the Nursing Home

Nonfiction
Chapbooks: A Historical Perspective
Staffordshire Figures: History in Earthenware 1740–1900
Photographic Cases: Victorian Design Sources 1840–1870
Staffordshire Animals: A Collector's Guide
Staffordshire Spaniels: A Collector's Guide
We Become By Being
The Silence and the Flame: Clare and Francis of Assisi
Counseling Gifted, Creative, and Talented Youth Through the Arts
A Creative Writing Companion

Author's Note

"Of Feathers, Of Flight" received a Merton Poetry of the Sacred Award (2007); "What Matters," "Of Feathers, Of Flight," "Confiteor," and "Whatever Might Pass for a Dream" were Paumanok Poetry Award finalists (2005 and 2006); and "The Trains" received an Allen Ginsberg Award (2006). "Like a Stone Falling" (titled "Alignment") was exhibited in "Double Exposures" at the Silconas Poetry Center & Art Gallery (January/March 2009)—my thanks to the judges and curators.

My sincerest gratitude to Renée Ashley for her excellent advice on the early manuscript, to Jan and P. C. Siegal for their special friendship, and to Charles DeFanti (long-time mentor, teacher, and friend), who continues generously to challenge and inspire me. My love and gratitude, always, to Alex Pinto, Bob Fiorellino, and Bijou Kenny, who share this collection's dedication.

For Alex, Bijou, and Bob

CONTENTS

III
WE DON'T FORGET

You do not need to know precisely what is happening,
or exactly where it is all going.
What you need is to recognize the possibilities and challenges
offered by the present moment, and to embrace them
with courage, faith and hope.

—THOMAS MERTON

PROLOGUE

This Living

It's not destination, but more what silence is when
you enter it deeply—like walking in snow (the hush
and spell). You have fallen your whole life to land
here (your long, exhausted sigh and only a stone
where love has left you: the minor key of it, the

pricked stars). You step back for perspective. Branches
move like voices; and just there, you hear the voice you
haven't heard in years (your own)—a kind of whistling
(what some call song). The leaves are astonished—
no shame in surprise, in anything moving or rooted—

it's what you get when you live long enough. So why
define what opened in your life or disappeared? You did
or didn't. And, yes, you remember how to live. The soul
does that. It's what moves you forward. (God and your
ghosts on the other side.) And here: this wing, this living.

I

WHERE MEMORY IS HOLY

Stars, Like Souls

When I was a child, my father made
sense of it. Orion tilted at his fingertips,
and he rocked Cassiopeia's chair with

hands so big I thought he would hold
me and all the stars forever. But stars,
like souls, step out of their bodies —
light more than light.

Tonight, frost burns the marigolds. A
last bird sings. I sit at my table and turn
a spoon sticky with sugar over and over

in my hands until my fingers shine the
way my father's did in that neighborhood
of stars, that world I believed was the
world without end.

The First Sorrow, How It Was

The day my father buried our dog,
the trees were giddy with wind
that seemed it would shake

our bones from our souls.
It rained so hard we couldn't see
from the kitchen window.

And when he came in,
shirt stuck to his back like
plastic-wrap, he wiped the dirt

from his shoes, his hands,
and sat with us at the table. His
chair, one leg short on the floor,

wobbled, so he stuck a matchbook
under it, and my mother said
something about fire. Grandma

said something about hell and
Callahan's wake, bagpipes wailing
like banshees, Callahan boxed and

ready to go. I was five years old,
prepared to die for a wake like that.
And, no, the sun didn't come out,

the sky stayed gray, but my father
sang—his own song, the one
about sun on the prairie; my mother

held my hand; and, determined not to
(even then), I didn't cry,
my next breath already taken.

The Music in It

For My Father

Concerning the music and the sky
that day, fretted by winter branches:
it wasn't Mendelssohn or any song I

knew but grief like percussion—not
from a distance—specific, slamming.
An hour earlier you walked the dog,

watched TV, dozed in your chair.
No time for thinning (the way
sound thins): in the crack between

air and breath, it was done. That fast—
your voice, the music in it, the way
it turned the corner before you.

Crooked Mercy

The crows came
to my mother's window,

black and flapping,
a month before she died.

I would have
pulled the curtain but

my mother, who had scattered
seed for scarlet cardinals,

motioned me close
and whispered *beautiful.*

Omens of nothing,
too late to mean more

than what they were,
they tilted back and forth

on the narrow ledge—
gestures without hands.

We took what was given:
a deathbed window's

outward arch, a crooked
mercy, the rush of wings.

A Darker Grace

Winter—trees in their leaf-night are
stark and black, talismans of a darker
grace. My mother loved them like this.
Humbled, she said, *but pure, so pure
you can see the shape of their bones.*

Winter—Christmas Eve; my mother
is dead. A band of carolers wanders
the streets like a ladder of sparrows.
Their song rinses and wrings the air.
I whisper some words, *O Holy Night*;

the carolers' voices bend with the road.
In the backyard, ivy clings to a stump
where the Rose of Sharon used to be.
It's stubborn, that ivy. Like the holly
we cut down, it keeps coming back; it

keeps on living, each green-veined leaf
a shoot from the stump of Jesse.
Up and down the street, white lights
twinkle and blink. The whole town
is star-scored, insensibly bright.

Black River

In the almost-dark of a late spring
evening, the air still holds a scent of
moss on dampened stone, the bitter
tang of bluebells.

You are with me because I remember
(the sense of you just over my left
shoulder), a shadow that follows
the light.

This was your place, where the world
should have let you go—here where
the river turns, a fishing pole in your
hand, the back of

your brown flannel shirt slipped from
your belt, your old shoes worn, as
they always were, on the insides
of their heels.

I have come to touch your death with
the palm of my hand, clench my fist
around it, and fling it upstream—
bone ash into space.

Go! Go now! I call down the stars
for your ransom. One by one they
fall into the river, which carries
them all away.

Of Feathers, Of Flight

...if I look up into the heavens I think that it will all come right...
and that peace and tranquility will return again.
         —ANNE FRANK

That spring, a baby jay fell from its nest,
 and we took it to Mrs. Levine, who told
us the mother would know our hands and
 never take it back. Spring that year was a

cardboard box, cries for eyedropper food—
 feather-stalks stretched into wings. We
knew, of course, that we couldn't keep it.
 (Later, we would mark the spot with stones

and twigs—where the bird fell, where we
 let it go—and sometimes, stopped in the
middle of play, would point and say, *there,*
 right there.) The day we freed it, it beat, a

heart-clock (wound and sprung in Ruth
 Levine's old hand) that, finally, finding
the sky, flew higher than all the briars
 strung like metal barbs above the fence—

a speck of updraft ash and gone. Heaven,
 fuller then for one small bird, spread its
blue wing over us and the tree and Mrs.
 Levine who, breathing deeply, raised her

numbered arm to the light and moved her
 thumb over each fingertip as if she could
feel to the ends of her skin the miracle
 edge of freedom, of feathers, of flight.

Snake Lady

She was the main event when
    the carnival came to town.
Fourteen and oh, so young,
    we stood inside her tent with
boys who spoke among themselves
    of things that made them men.

Had we been older, we might
    have understood—their helpless
fascination as the snake slid
    between her breasts and made its
thick descent along her thighs.
    Those boys never blinked until
her fingers stroked the coils

straight, tightened on the head,
    and coaxed it to a sudden milky
venom. With an innocence we
    didn't think we had, we blushed
and turned from the sure and
    easy way she made them burn.

Where Memory Is Holy

Not nearly as large as memory believes, this
    is the front-porch place of my childhood, a
cinder block bag of cracked ceilings and
    long windows, a side-street fortress of shingle
and stone. This is the house where my mother
    came into the world and left it, where radiators
knocked into night and the shadows of five
    generations beat like bat wings behind the walls.
How long my father lamented, *this goddamn*
    house — worms in the window frames, holes in
the roof. Oh house, the wrecking ball swings,
    the jackhammer waits, but memory is holy
and the earth too shallow to hold your bones.

The Sap Bush

It was like this every spring, the pathway
right about here, a tangle of brush that led
between pines to the stand of maples we
called the Sap Bush.

There was sugar deep inside those trees
and we pressed our hands to the bark,
convinced that we felt it. After the nozzles
were driven in

and the tin pails hung, we went back at
night, to that place where stars pressed
their imprimatur against the dark. Cold
in our warm bodies,

we stood in the trees' deep shadows and
wished ourselves up, into that other universe
of gradual light. I imagine us there, called
back in middle age

to a language of stars that was larger than
logic and never quite lost—hands pressed
to the trees, we feel the sap still flowing.
Thick. Golden. Sweet.

Another Autumn

This is the story: joy at the heart of things,
flame at the center. And more grief than
we bargained for. Leaf-rot rolls its hoop

through colder air, life becomes breakable.
The roses are gaunt in their tightening skin;
downtown, chrysanthemums everywhere.

A vagrant wraps his feet in newsprint.
Most people pass without looking.
It's like that here where I moved to a

"better" life. In my old, down-at-the-mouth
town, the boys all knew where they were
headed—sweat, and the smell of it.

It was harder for the girls (what we wanted):
a house, children to fill it, husbands with
hands less worn than our fathers'.

Up on Milton Avenue, rich kids played
tennis at the Ilderan Club. Sometimes we
mimicked them, wiggled our butts, swung

our arms, and yelled *Love!* because *we*
knew exactly what that meant. Our dreams
didn't talk tennis, but even the girls could

step up to the plate at Flanagan's Field and
swing the bat as if we were taking hits at
a life in which singles were more credible

than home runs. There were things we
didn't ask for, things we forgave — the
trees on fire, and not enough rain.

In Rain

This is the way the hours go:
the long rain changes from
torrent to drizzle to torrent.
It pools on the windowsills,
blurs the azaleas — dogwoods
float like watered silks.

In England, I walked in rain
like this over cobbled roads
to a ruined cathedral where
pilgrims crawled through
centuries of penance. In
the dark chancel, where the

last offices were chanted, I
stood with the ghosts of
hooded monks and vanished
Saxons, and then I knelt. Knees
pressed to a hollowed stone, I
worshipped the perfect silence.

East Rahway

The past is a foreign country,
            they do things differently there.
                                    — L. P. Hartley

All it takes is something familiar: the shape of a
hand or a stranger's eyes in the sudden light of
a theater when the movie ends. Then, something
deep in memory's birthwood calls me back.
The past is my first language, a speakable grace.

On summer nights in East Rahway, our fathers
sat on front porches in worn t-shirts, their
calloused hands wrapped around beer cans as
the last stars took their places like nail-heads
on a dark and holy board. Inside, our mothers

sang as they washed the dinner dishes, and we
went to sleep with the easy grace of children.
All of our grandmothers spoke with accents,
rolled their stockings down to their ankles like
nylon UFOs, and people shouted at them when

they spoke, enunciating carefully, as if our
grandmothers weren't only foreign but deaf.
Different from the beginning, we were the city's
middle children, never as tough as the kids from
the projects, and only half as cool as the kids who

lived behind the high school on the other side
of town. Cut off from the rest of Rahway, we
lived between Route 1 and Linden Airport, in
a place where sleep was rubbed out of night to
the sound of trucks stumbling over potholes

and propjets taking off on runway number three.
Safe in our own society, we lived a little religion
of unlikely saints whose blood offerings were
elbows and knees that scraped like autumn
leaves on the sidewalks. In East Rahway, hardly

anyone died or went away. Those were the days
before we knew what *dead* meant. But when
Mr. Malone, who lived in the corner house,
did it, the bagpipes wailed and skirled for
three days in his living room, a hundred octaves

higher than all the blades of grass we ever
held between our thumbs and blew against—
a different kind of party. There were no soccer
games, no little league, no one drove us anywhere.
We walked to the corner store and hiked down

Lower Road to Merck's Creek, the mosquitoed
water stained even then by chemicals we couldn't
name; but, oh, the bright and oily rings that spread
above the stones we skipped like shivering circles
of mercury. There were forests then, across the

street, and deep. We were wood nymphs and
Druids, foreign legionnaires led by my cousin
Eddie. Soldiers of whatever fortune was, we
followed into the hymned and scrawling weeds—
the underbrush belled by our footsteps, trees

tuned to prodigal birds. We were Arthur and
Guinevere, Merlin, Morgan, all the knights, and
one Rapunzel who lost her hair in a bubble gum
accident. We did things differently then, believed
in summer's synonymous sun, December's

piebald light, white-maned and glistening, the
moon above us, cloud-ribbed in semi-silhouette.
The past falls like water from winter boots.
Merck's Creek, darker, dirtier with new pollution,
moves more slowly. The streets, once so wide

and willing, are smaller. And the forest is gone,
the initials we carved lost with fallen trees,
the green spirits laid to rest beneath a block of
factories. But, still, if you cross Route 1 on
a night overworked with summer stars, and

stand on the corner of Scott and Barnett, you
will find our fathers there. Kents and Winstons
burn, beer cans shine in the baritone heat. Our
mothers and grandmothers sing, ghostly soloists,
eggshell voices—reedy, thin. And *we* are there,

lips pressed smugly on chocolate cigarettes; our
pockets ring with Pez candies. Listen! A child's
voice calls *Excalibur* into the night, those old bones
still in the road—skull and neck, a few vertebrae
that we tossed like dice to tell our future.

The Trains

We felt them first. Fingers pressed to the rails,
    a dull rumble filled our hands and hummed into
our arms before the cone of light, the great clatter

of metal against metal. Trestled high, above the
    bridge on Grand Avenue, we knew those tracks
went on forever, between trees that lined the ties

like stations of the cross. The hill was forbidden but
    holy, thick with clover, ripe with berries in spring.
The year I was nine, an April blizzard swept the

sky and we went to the trains in the dark. The wires
    strummed into sparks, the rails were a dazzle of
shadows. Our faces—ghosts of our selves—reflected

in every train car window, lines of breath etched in
    passing glass. Above us, chimney smoke hung like
smears of candle grease among the clouds.

We were grubby and poor, but we believed. We said
    our prayers, ate fish on Fridays, and never rode
those trains. We could only kneel in something like

wonder, something like praise, and wait for the
    tracks' reverent shudder. The memory is a gauze
engine that time blows through and keeps me small.

II

SOMEHOW THE ANGEL

Like a Stone Falling

But suddenly you're anyone's to take apart,
put back together—this time you know too
much, and you listen for a voice (half-feeling,
half-remembered) that calls to you the way
your mother's voice called you home.

You become the brush of a curtain's hem, the
birds' sawblade wings—the band on your wrist
so tightly tied its mark defines the skin—a small,
strict history. You know what the body creates
and erases—the lushness, the vacancies.

One dark slips through another. And sound—
like a stone falling. Like the dead throwing
stones. Knotted rope in the knotted tree. No
sound for that. Pines. Sky. Notion of sun—
the world spins in its dazzle.

Where Lightning Strikes

There's no translation for the terror
when the surgeon says *I have bad
news,* on the phone, no less, and me
alone, a glass baton that someone
else is twirling. What I wanted was

glisten and shine, but in the space
between sip and swallow, the front
door's flap and click, it is this,

explicitly this: no illusion of control,
a bird startled by the sudden sky, not
ready for Heaven. Suddenly furious

(and that a blessing), I think *death* —
that bastard, his hand on my breast, his
lips at my ear, his tongue clicking...

Call the fear *it is what it is* (ratchet-
hand, goat's foot) — a kind of running.
And that starling on the fence (wing-
flick and spliced song), the flat field
where lightning strikes the tower.

What She Thinks When She Thinks Death

Here it is—the click and clatter—the world shaken,
the sack of rocks. Here is the fast light of it. The dead
lined up and looking in—their hinged hands hard; the
river a white knuckle behind them. She gathers their
graves like coals and fire. Night leans in on long legs.
Survival, she thinks, *is anything that doesn't break us.*

What It Will Take

I

If only the barn that leans into
sunset were permanent—old
shingle eye and battered siding—
this fear less scrupulous.

II

At dusk, deer feed in a corner
of the field; heads low, they
nibble grass. Winter's hunger
is close. Above them a dark
shape circles and waits, eyes

fixed on the warmth below.
The deer know. Call it instinct,
call it gift. The smallest sound
and they scatter. They know
what will save them.

III

I pull the sides of my jacket
close, check my pockets for
tissues and keys, familiar things,
still there.

In Which

There are fifty rooms in the
cancer center, the waiting room
always full—all of us waiting.
The nurses ask for dates of birth
and know us by those numbers.

A few remember my name.
Today, it took four tries before
the chemo nurse found a vein that
didn't collapse. I'm exhausted.
My dogs follow me back to bed.

It doesn't matter to them that I
wear a wig, false eyelashes, my
eyebrows penciled in. The boy-dog
touches my face with his paw when
I wake. If I move now, he'll press

himself close, his sister closer to
him. Something sings outside my
window—birds or scraps of stars
(if stars can sing at all). Clouds
shift and drift. What to what?

I'm told the odds are in my favor;
but it's simpler than that—the cure
works or it doesn't. I imagine a
stone, it's slow wearing down, the
light in which it casts no shadow.

Another Night on the Wing of That Dream

It's the same damned dream—a hole and she
knows she's in it. She feels herself flail, small

(like *shiver*, the bed sprung with the weight of
her life). She can't lift off. She flaps, arms

pitched like wings (that would be bird—wren,
sparrow—but she isn't). She races and revs, gains

a fraction, then bumps down (the way one fall
bumps into another). She thinks: *a spade for the*

feathers, a bucket for the blood (whatever is left—
her own slow ghost). But stop! The fortune-teller

trips—illusion, trick—there's one bird left on
the water, one wing through, and it's rising.

Somehow the Angel

It happens like this: the sudden waking,
your heart skipped and flipped, lungs
strung like pebbles on wire; and that
next breath—you're sure you can't take it,
but you *do* breathe.

You think *sleep*, and not sleep. You think
about pills, about taking *all* the pills—
what that would mean, where you would
be if you weren't here—and you
almost consider it.

Always, then, the old angel wheezes in.
Not quite luminous, never on his knees,
his wings creak, beat at oblique angles
(all that flapping—it's hardly celestial),
but his own

weight escapes him, and he flies toward
you, wrists like bells ringing, a miracle in
each fist. You say you believe (though
you know you talk to yourself)—you
believe in anything

with wings, no cage to hold it, and it's
okay, it's okay—the angel walks you up
the stairs. Over the trash bin. Dumpster.
And, somehow, somehow, you pull
yourself through.

Almost

Think of it this way: a shadow flicks at your vision's edge —
 a sudden something that resembles light. A wild swan
crosses the pond, scatters the moon and disappears. Think
 of Leda, the great wings beating, the staggering girl —
how much you survive (how grief lets go). Someone drags
 a stone across the fence that separates the street from
pond and swan. The sound rattles and rings — far from the
 sea, from the stone circle (perimeter, edge), where you
walked (then). Your dogs, breathless from running rabbits
 and weeds, sit at your feet, heads cocked, ready for home.
A small brown bird sings in its sleep, and (look at you) —
 you are almost happy.

No Word for It

It wasn't the twilight silence,
the heron's glide and dive,
wings part of the sky;

raindrops that plucked her
sleeves like fingers, or wind
that hauled a cargo of clouds;

what she might have called
longing, though perhaps,
precisely, there's no word

for it—a door that opens
inward, and she's
walking through.

Shadow

She holds her shadow,
      turns it in her hand,
            spins it left and right,
                  watches it split
                        deep down and far

back until each dark
      glyph shines in the
            light. It is *her* shadow
                  cut from the whole
                      (cut new as often as

she must) the way,
      as a child, she cut
            paper dolls—strings
                  of them—each one
                      unfolding another.

And Nothing Less

Unaccustomed to that door
and its slamming, they are

hesitant at first, but persistent.
They crease the dark and work

off the light like airborne starlings
sprung from a nest that hope still

dares to inhabit. Explicit as air,
articulate as breath and nothing

less, her dreams want her back.
They drag their wings into flight

and pull her up with them—so
of this life and being in it—intent

on the shaping of things, the road's
bent knee, the long way home.

That Much Closer

No big epiphanies,
but smaller things
I'm more aware of:

moths that call the
porch light a party,
my dogs asleep on

pillows beside me,
their sleepy breath
warm on my hand;

and this morning a
neighbor's child
balanced on her knees

where the crook of
the apple tree flattens.
Hands outstretched,

she sings what she
knows from Handel's
Messiah—*alleluia*,

alleluia—again and
again, her woodwind
voice through branches

and just as high, that
much closer to God—
the sky in her arms.

Counting the Change

Perhaps life is just that…a dream and a fear.
— JOSEPH CONRAD

Five souls in transit fly past the window;
their arms lap air like dry tongues—clouds
in their hair, sky thrown from their fingers;

they don't have wings and carry fault like
thousand-pound weights—anonymous bodies
(still in their skin)—the road below,

mountains to clear, and nothing shaped like
heaven. No directions from here to there,
the flight path narrow, the light idle; but

they all hang on; they count the change left
in their pockets, and tell themselves that
surely, by now, the admission is paid.

This

She calls it hope, keeps the
smallest holiness close, anything
touchable; though at times, like
hearsay (peripheral), she names

herself in the second or third
person—a way of distancing, a
way of seeing. Pain has become
a smaller word, spoken from a

distance. She makes peace with
what is and there *is* peace (the
way things are). Forgetting is
this: a sustainable silence.

She never says what the breast
cancer did (her mirror's lesser
reflection, and what stays broken).
She *is* what remains—sorrow

and self (the long and the bell
of it), the easiness that is not (all
things considered) hers—the
backward step, the step ahead.

Survivor

A jay on the fence preaches to a
squirrel. I watch the squirrel quiver,
the way squirrels do—its whole
body flickers. I'm not sure why this
reminds me of when I was five and

something died in our drain spout.
Feather or fur, I watched my father
dig it out, knowing (as a child knows)
how much life matters. I have seen how
easily autumn shakes the yellow leaves,

how winter razes the shoals of heaven.
I have felt love's thunder and moan, and
had my night on the wild river. I have
heard the cancer diagnosis with my name
in it. I know what mercy is and isn't.

Morning breaks from sparrows' wings
(life's breezy business), and I'm still here,
still in love with the sorrows, the joys—
days like this, measured by memory, the
ticking crickets, the pulse in my wrist.

III

WE DON'T FORGET

Lag Time

Every morning is like the morning that
came before. Light shreds through matted
clouds, grass bent where your shadow
crossed it. It may be hot, or a breeze
blows through. It rains, or sunlight slides
down the side of your house. No promises
broken or kept, you settle into your own
absence—no story or more than you're
willing to tell, and it comes to you—
how it happens, what stillness is.

Confiteor

"But this mutability—what is it? Is it soul? Is it body?"

       – St. Augustine, *Confessions*, Book Twelve, Chapter VI

Imagine Icarus before the air let go,
before the sea lunged up. Imagine the

downward pitch, the boy wing-tipped
and sticky. Of course he failed, we all

fail. Things come unglued. And not
surprising—this mutability of mutable

things. The way Brueghel painted it,
life goes on: ploughman, shepherd,

oblivious sheep. Life goes on: the
garden passes its shadow to the fence;

birds murmur and settle their wings
like prayers spoken in hopeless places.

The earth curves into place. Water. Silt.
Sky. The moon rises and keeps on rising.

And Is

Spring, greening and winged, sets
buds on the lilac. Dewdrops fall on
the spider's web, small acclamations—
accessible, real. This is the world,
flung from the sun's infallible fist, an
arrangement of light that praises the
wonder of substance.

In the forest, new leaves take the
place of fallen elms. A river splits
the creased ravine—such distance
between the rocks and sky. High
above the rippling eddies, a voice
that's barely heard belongs to you,
to all that is, and is.

Whatever Might Pass for a Dream

The trocheed tick of the mantle
clock is trained on the coming
hour, tomorrow already taking
shape. It's mid-summer and years
ago, relentless heat on both sides

of my pillow. At Warananco Park,
my father holds me under fireworks,
skyburst and boom while I sleep.
The vision shifts, my mother and
father dance beneath a willow gone

in the storm of '56. Someone is
singing. The sound is breathy, is
misty, is sweet. Fitful and faint, a
night cricket rubs its forelegs together,
the first pale bird warbles and weeps.

Coming and Going

Evening pulls the sky-rim down.
    Clouds wait for the wind.

The river fills with lights from the
    farthest shore. The day has

been long; you are tired. You count
    your losses, the wounds that

are yourself. A freight train whistles
    in the distance, hollow, October-

boned—a myth slipped from the
    flinty sky. Its remote chugging

gathers force, coming and going
    like a wing, like a star.

Once These Names

Light shifts past the faceless names
and catches at the corners of the stones.

Once these names were shadows with
substance, as we are, flesh and bone.

Near a tomb in the next row, thistle
splits; seed tufts float above the river.

Ghosts gather, a dim procession, like
images left on the retina after a dream.

I shiver against you — no love without
loss. And no guarantee against memory.

Leaves turn their undersides up, a sign of
rain. A wild bird pauses between songs.

You kiss my hand in exchange for
the sorrow and say: *This isn't us.*

Where They Are Now

Ubi sunt qui ante nos fuerunt?

Are they there in that place where
stars and human hearts begin? Were
there God-shaped hills to guide them
toward light? A sympathetic angel to
lead the way? Was it as simple as
opening their eyes, unstartled,
unblinking, in a luminous room?
Do they remember the moon's half-
face and full, the deep sky trestled
with clouds or marked with stars?
Do they still know the river—windbud,
thorn, and the way skin feels?
Have they been transfigured or risen
faceless, their hands too vague, too
shapeless, to hold? And if there is
music, does any refrain tug memory
toward the tattered screen door, the
way its hinges creaked as it shut,
softly, behind them?

Tending the Graves

The snow has melted, the stream remembers
how to be a stream. In the distance, Canada geese
rise from the river and lift their migration away

from the world, a raw symbolism that stops us
for a moment. We shade our eyes from the sun

as the geese veer west — a wavy vee that
crosses clouds, enters, and disappears.
We get on with the conscious option of doing,

pull away leaves and tangled ivy, thrust our
fingers into earth, and know what lies beneath.

In Memory Of

(After Dante Gabriel Rossetti's *Beata Beatrix*)

No movement but this: subdued luminosity, sunlight
from the distant city. River. Bridge. There is always
a background (that far, this close), and what memory
does—like the dusky lines of a double shadow,
it multiplies loss.

In Rossetti's *Beata*, a sundial casts its metal wing
on the thin, blown hour when leaving begins.
Red dove, white poppy: the woman, transfixed,
slips—diffused like light through darkened glass—
her hands open and soft.

I am here and you aren't. It is summer—
the sky is clapper and bell, the lemonade sweet.
I can almost hear you singing. In that voice
without margin, the notes I remember most
are high and low.

Selling the Family House

I didn't plan to be undone
by a catbird crying, irises in
bloom where a cherry tree stood,
the baby, born dead, buried there;

or those ovals on the wall where
our pictures were hung, holes
from the nails that held them.

The house—empty or nearly
empty—crumbles into itself.
I leave a few books on their shelf.
Some shimmer, the others are rags.

What voice do I hear (or want to
hear)? The catbird cries; the earth
turns on wing-boned fingers.

Watching

In Memory of Yeatsy
(January 5, 1993–July 6, 2008)

The way his head slips from
my hand as I lay him down,
his eyes still open (though I
try to close them), the same
warmth still in his small body.

It is this: death, a skill learned
by those who observe it; grief
what we keep—and memory
always, at least in part, about
forgetting. I cross his paws the
way he crossed them in sleep.

Like all deaths that summer
remembers, I walk his home.
A patch of sun climbs the stairs
without him; white moths,
like snowflakes, span the sky.

What Grief Comes To

For Les

A different light follows the fields.
Hawthorn blossoms whiten the earth—
delicate, brief—like snow on water.
There are badgers in the wood, the

swallows home and nesting. Life,
as you said, *is*—with or without us;
you were gone before this bright
blooming, your room dark, the

kennel empty. I want to tell you
about the peonies, the evening air
tipped with scent, everything green.
Friend, I understand your grief

and what it came to—no moral or
metaphor, only the absolute truth
of that moment: the step ladder
placed, the rope in your hand.

Like I Said

Okay, so it's Sunday. I didn't
go to church. I'm an Irish Catholic,
I know about sin, but I was tired and
just didn't feel like getting dressed.

On Thursday night, I fell and broke
a slat from the garden fence. My
hip still hurts—the bruise is as big
as my Yorkie's head.

That would have been enough, but
this morning the vacuum coughed up
a hairball and quit. The only food in
the fridge is a bearded yogurt.

The washing machine refuses to spin.
There's no clean underwear left, so
I'm not wearing any. Like I said,
I was tired; I didn't feel like getting

dressed, so I didn't go to church and
abdicated rights to all that grace.
I put on a pair of dirty jeans, a dirty
shirt, and sat outdoors all morning.

I did nothing but talk to my dogs,
watch squirrels, and wonder what it
might be like to nibble Prozac from
Johnny Depp's lower lip.

It's What

It's not all nocturnes and willows, she says,
it's not all blood.

It's what the mystics teach — what you don't
hold onto, what you

don't keep (these words, this dust). It's what
you know is truth,

what keeps you focused: one eye dark,
light in the other...

Of Other

It isn't now or this patch of blue autumn,
light skimmed like milk without substance
(its ghost on my lips). Or the way trees darken

before the sky, the way light slants through
pines (my neighbor's lamp or the moon).
It's not the way night feels when I walk in

March, when snow melts into mud, and I
smell grass again; when I know, without seeing,
that tight buds open high in the branches. It's

not the expected order of things but moments of
other (when something startles you into knowing
something other), and the heaviness lifts inside you.

Tonight, wind pulled leaves from the sky
to my feet and, suddenly (without warning) a
deer leapt from the thicket behind me — leapt

and disappeared — past me as I passed myself,
my body filled with absence, with air,
a perfect mold of the light gone through it.

What Matters

We are what the dead remember. They have no
dream of their own, but cradle us like violins,

close to the throat, close to the bone. They
dream of earth and dirt, and come to us in the

dark (anxious, hungry), hands wrung like breaths
from their bodies — it is not for them to leave

us completely, to remove themselves from our
partial light. They have something to tell us:

what matters is the quiet beak of a lark in the seed,
the dead tree's shadow that stretches upstream.

We Don't Forget

Tonight you heard my
footsteps in the room

above and called to me.
I didn't answer. There
was only the movement of

air my body made when
I turned to your voice.

Later, in what might have
been a dream, a little boy
played stickball in the street,

the moon shuffled home.
Grace is acceptance—

all of it, whatever is—as
in we live for this: love
and gratitude enough.

We don't forget
how it feels to rejoice.

About the Author

Adele Kenny is the author of twenty-three books (poetry and nonfiction). Her poems, reviews, and articles have been published in journals worldwide, and her poems have appeared in books and anthologies published by Crown, Tuttle, Shambhala, and McGraw-Hill. She is the recipient of numerous awards for her poetry, including two fellowships from the New Jersey State Council on the Arts, a first-place Merit Book Award, a Thomas Merton Poetry of the Sacred Award, and a Writer's Digest Poetry Award. A former professor of creative writing in the College of New Rochelle's Graduate School, she is the founding director of the Carriage House Poetry Series and poetry editor of *Tiferet*.

Website: http://mysite.verizon.net/adelekenny/
Poetry Blog: http://adelekenny.blogspot.com/